SPIRITUAL
FOOD *for the*
Soul

SPIRITUAL FOOD *for the* Soul

I AM THE BREAD OF LIFE:

HE THAT COMETH TO ME SHALL NEVER HUNGER

JOHN 6:35 KJV

ROCHELLE WILLIAMS

ISBN: 979-8-9909003-6-3 *(paperback)*
        979-8-9909003-7-0 *(hardback)*
        979-8-9909003-8-7 *(epub)*

All Scripture quotations are taken from the King James Version. Public domain.

Editing, formatting and cover design by
ChristianEditingAndDesign.com.

I share this book with the loves of my life and biggest supporters, my husband and daughters. Thank you for believing in me and taking this journey with me to write this spiritual book as a beacon of light and symbol of hope. We have always said that God's Word has the power to change the world. Your love for me and faith in me propelled me to do God's will.

James, Candice, Constance, & Queenie(grand dog)

In Loving Memory of
my beloved parents, James & Lillie Ross, and my beloved
father-in-law and spiritual father, Alvin Williams.

Your legacy is etched into our hearts and minds,
and we will cherish your love forever. You gave
so much of yourselves to make life better for so
many. Rest in heaven, our dear parents.

Much love to my dear Mother Juanita Williams and family members and church family.

A special thank you to Dixie Phillips and Clayton Jones for their editing expertise and to the staff at Christian Editing and Design for their editorial assistance and support in bringing my book to existence. I personally want to thank Dixie, my spiritual friend and co-author of our poem, "Peace Be Still," for her support and prayers from the beginning to the finished product.

Contents

Spiritual Seasoning

As you read these inspirational words and Scriptures, I pray you will be encouraged to see the love of God. I pray you will be the example for others because the world needs to see His light and love. The only light that can devour darkness is God's love. It shines through His people. Thus, I urge you to go light up the world with His love.

In this chapter, the word *seed* is an allegory of God's image and fruit of the Spirit. The image of the seed illustrates the characteristics of Jesus Christ that inhabit the life of believers through the power of the Holy Spirit. In turn, believers grow spiritually and draw others to Christ. Just as seeds are essential to nourishing life by what they develop and bring forth, the fruit of the Spirit is essential to nourishing the life of a believer and follower of Jesus Christ. Furthermore, seeds are a symbol of life and beauty. They were established from the very beginning by our heavenly Father, the Creator of life and beauty.

God's seeds give life, and they beautify His people in righteousness. Sowing the "good seeds" of the Spirit is rewarded with beautiful fruits that grow from the everlasting tree of the Spirit.

The beautiful, peculiar tree is a chosen tree of God. It is planted in a special place so it can produce good, prosperous fruit. It is symbolic of God's peculiar people, who are chosen by Him. They are connected to the body of Christ to glorify Him and shine like heavenly stars—like the brightness of the heavens. God's Word confirms this truth:

> For a good tree bringeth not forth corrupt fruit; neither doth a corrupt tree bring forth good fruit. For every tree is known by his own fruit.... A good man out of the good treasure of his heart bringeth forth that which is good; and an evil man out of the evil treasure of his heart bringeth forth that which is evil. (Luke 6:43–45)

The tree is known by its fruit just as every believer is known by his or her fruit. Each piece of fruit is unique and significant. We are important to God. He wants us to love and serve Him as well as love and serve His fellow man.

CHAPTER 1

Be a Beautiful, Peculiar Tree

And he shall be like a tree
planted by the rivers of
water, that bringeth forth
his fruit in his season; his
leaf also shall not wither;
and whatsoever he doeth
shall prosper. (Psalm 1:3)

As CHRISTIANS, GOD GIVES US DIVINE INNER SEEDS. In time, these seeds will flourish into beautiful, peculiar trees planted for the world to see His glory. Although these seeds require cultivation and care, they are already established on a solid foundation in His Word and His Son, Jesus Christ. These seeds are manifested within us. They build character, portray God's image, and give light to the world. As we live on this earth and walk this Christian journey, we must take these God-given seeds and implant them in the hearts and minds of others to propagate in the world. We must sow these seeds according to the Word of God in order to develop and produce good results like the tree that brings forth good fruit planted by the rivers of water.

One of the most powerful divine seeds God gives to us is the seed of love. Love is mysterious, so we might ask, "Why God's love? Why would He give us this seed?" It is because love was in the beginning: everything that God is, all that He created, and all that He gave to human life is because He is love. He loves us.

Each one of us was created in His image of love. God gives love because He is the epitome of love and He created us out of love. The Bible clearly teaches that love is the essence of God:

And we have known and believed the love that God hath to us. God is love; and he that dwelleth in love dwelleth in God, and God in him. (1 John 4:16)

The highest form of love is God's divine love displayed through His Son, Jesus Christ. This goes for the whole world. God sent His only Son to be the propitiation for our sins. God's love is perfect, immeasurable, and pure. It never falters and never fails. God gives love because He gave His best to save the world. Consider the following:

For God so loved the world, that he gave his only begotten Son, that whosoever believeth in him should not perish, but have everlasting life. (John 3:16)

The beauty of the love of Jesus Christ is that He left heaven, took on flesh, and came into the world He created. Jesus Christ demonstrated this kind of divine love to His Father and to all humanity in the way He lived and died for the sins of us all:

And the Word was made flesh, and dwelt among us, (and we beheld his glory, the glory as of the only begotten of the Father,) full of grace and truth. (John 1:14)

The Word made flesh is God demonstrating His best to humanity. God gives us His very best. He gives love because the greatest of all is love. His Word teaches that charity or love is the ultimate gift:

> And now abideth faith, hope, charity, these three; but the greatest of these is charity. (1 Corinthians 13:13)

We can be endowed with all that the world has to offer, but without love, we have no true connection to God. Indeed, we are nothing without Him and His love. God gives love because it is not just a gift, but it is the first and greatest commandment:

> Master, which is the great commandment in the law? Jesus said unto him, Thou shalt love the Lord thy God with all thy heart, and with all thy soul, and with all thy mind. (Matthew 22:36–37)

God wants us to love Him wholeheartedly—putting Him first above all things. He is a jealous God, which is why He makes a point to instruct us to love Him, but also one another. We see this clearly in the following Scripture:

> Beloved, let us love one another: for love is of God; and every one that loveth is born of God, and knoweth God. (1 John 4:7)

Love is the key to knowing Him. Hence, the only way we can change the world and reach each other is through brotherly love. The Bible is adamant that anyone who doesn't show love for his brother does not truly know God:

> He that loveth not knoweth not God; for God is love. (1 John 4:8)

God gives love because love covers a multitude of sins. His love is abundant:

> And above all things have fervent charity among yourselves: for charity shall cover the multitude of sins. (1 Peter 4:8)

God's love covers our faults and restores us when we have sinned. Besides, God tells us that He will forgive our sins and remember them no more.

A Great Love Story of God's Love

The Bible shares numerous illustrations of God's love and forgiveness. A great example is found in the Old Testament—the book of Hosea. The prophet Hosea depicts the nature of God's love, forgiveness, and redemption. Gomer, the wife of Hosea, represents God's people of Israel, who were disobedient to His commandments and unfaithful by worshipping idols. The story is illustrative of wounded and redemptive love. This is depicted by the marriage of a husband and wife, which is symbolic of the love, unity, and redemption God has for

His people. Despite the infidelity of Israel, God's infinite love and mercy overshadowed their sins. His union with His people is as the Bridegroom with His Bride. God is faithful with His love and long-suffering with His people.

The meaning of the story is centered around Hosea's obedience. Although Hosea was commanded by God to marry Gomer—a harlot—he did not understand the plan God had for him. At any rate, Hosea did as God instructed. Above and beyond, Hosea did as God instructed out of obedience as God was showing Hosea the mystery of His love—even when people do wrong against you. Furthermore, Hosea's marriage and relationship with Gomer is a great example of the covenantal relationship God had with Israel. Hosea's marriage to a harlot symbolizes Israel's unfaithfulness to God by following other gods and disobeying the commandments. In essence God was saying, "I know that My people, the Israelites, have sinned against Me and have rejected Me just like Gomer rejects you, but I love My people and want them to return to Me. I will forgive their sins. You must love Gomer and forgive her sins."

Hosea did what God asked even though there was a stigma attached to Gomer. Despite Gomer's promiscuous lifestyle, Hosea married her out of obedience to God.

Hosea was a faithful husband and Gomer was an unfaithful wife—she strayed from her wedding vows. She was with other men; in turn, her relationship with Hosea was broken. Hosea's spirit must have been crushed and his heart shattered. He must have felt his marriage was beyond reconciliation because of Gomer's betrayal.

Just as Gomer was unfaithful to Hosea, the Israelites were disobedient and unfaithful to God. They rejected God and worshipped idols. They sinned against God despite the love He had shown them. The unfaithfulness of God's children must have broken His heart, but God's love covers a multitude of sins. He willingly offers forgiveness:

> And their sins and iniquities will I remember no more. (Hebrews 10:17)

We may endure painful situations, but God's grace enables us to forgive and reconcile. For example, when Gomer got into trouble and was on the slave auction block, God told Hosea to go get his wife. Hosea obeyed God and followed God's plan for his life. Hosea had to redeem Gomer for fifteen pieces of silver and a homer and a half of barley.

These events prompt the following questions: Did Gomer deserve to be redeemed? Did the children of Israel deserve to be redeemed? Do we deserve to be redeemed when we reject God and disobey His Word? It is easy to agree one does not deserve redemption when one rejects God. After all, we should be thankful God doesn't give us what we deserve. God doesn't treat us as our transgressions or sins deserve. He is slow to anger and always abounding in love.

Look at God's Love

God taught Hosea about His great love. God also must teach us. Oftentimes, we don't understand God's plan for our lives, but God will always order our steps in the right path. He will equip us with everything we need in order to do His will, yet we must recognize it. For example, through the story of Hosea, God showed His love for the children of Israel and declared to keep that covenant regardless of their disobedience. Hosea was equipped with open arms—just like when God told Israel He would forgive their sins and love His people freely. He wanted them to obey His voice and follow Him so they would be a blessed and model nation for all nations to see His goodness. By the same token, God wants us to be blessed and not cursed. God wants us to obey His Word. He loves us so much He forgives our sins when we repent. He welcomes us back into His fold and He remembers our sins no more.

What Does Love Do?

Love overshadows hate. Love is the Spirit of God. Hate is the spirit of Satan. God has all power over Satan, and love conquers evil. God's light defeats darkness. Love has all power in His hands. Consider the following Scripture:

> And Jesus came and spake unto them, saying, All power is given unto me in heaven and in earth. (Matthew 28:18)

Love is the most powerful force there is. Love forgives, and God forgives us and teaches us to forgive the transgressions of those who have wounded us. Furthermore, forgiveness is a weapon every believer needs to have in their arsenal:

> For if ye forgive men their trespasses, your heavenly Father will also forgive you. (Matthew 6:14)

As Christians, we must embody God's seed of love and sow it everywhere we go. Sowing love doesn't just mean just speaking kind words, but we must earnestly and sincerely show in action mercy, forgiveness, long-suffering, and patience just like God shows us. Sure, there are many other God-given seeds, but start with love–the greatest of all. As mentioned above, love was in the beginning and will live forever. These seeds will make you more like the Lord. They will stamp His image on your heart. You will become what He wants you to be. When you sow these seeds, you will light up the world with hope. You will be like a beautiful, peculiar tree planted by the rivers of water that prospers and brings forth good fruit.

What Does This Mean to Us Today?

God's love gives meaning to life, and it will never die. His love is divine and the key to living a blessed life built on the foundation of love—Jesus Christ. It is unshakeable and rooted in the Word of God. Without love, life fails. We fail and never fulfill God's will for our life. Love builds a home. Love brings people together. Love forgives and reconciles. Love lends a helping hand. Love does not harm. Love gives life. Give someone fresh hope and life by showing them the love they so desperately are searching for. Go light up your corner of the world with God's love.

Our Prayer

Heavenly Father,

Thank You for Your seed of love. It is the foundation of all authentic love. It's the reason You created life and gave Your only Son to redeem us. Without love, we cannot please You. For Your Word tells us that anyone who does not love does not know You because You are love. Without Your Agape love, we cannot truly love our brethren. Without Your love, we cannot conquer hate. Only Your love can do that. Without Your love, there is no forgiveness. Only Your love can give us the courage and strength to forgive. Without Your love, there is no peace. Without Your love, we cannot experience Your presence. Your love is the shining light this broken world needs. Jesus, You are the Light of the world. Help us, Father, to light up the world with Your love. Thank You, Father, for Your love. It truly is the greatest of all. In Jesus's Name we pray.

Amen.

Spiritual Seasoning

As revealed throughout the Holy Bible, God manifested His works and divine power in unusual ways to get the attention of His people. He did this to preserve and prevent them from walking into a life of darkness, destruction, and ultimately death. God does not want us to fall under the curses of disobedience, nor does He desire for us to perish. He does, however, want us all to come to repentance. God wants us to love Him and serve Him and be obedient to His Word. If we fully submit our will to God's will, He promised to "open to thee His good treasure . . . and to bless all the work of thine hand" (Deuteronomy 28:12).

God is patient and forgiving. He is plenteous in mercy because He loves us; furthermore, He is "faithful and just to forgive us our sins, and to cleanse us from all unrighteousness" (1 John 1:9). God needs us to be His hands and feet and to do His will and to be witnesses for Him to reach the world.

CHAPTER 2

If a Donkey Can See, Why Can't We?

And the Lord opened the mouth of the ass, and she said unto Balaam, What have I done unto thee, that thou hast smitten me these three times? (Numbers 22:28)

G OD CAN PUT HIS DIVINE POWER INTO ACTION BY SIMPLY SPEAKING, USING HIS HANDS, OR UTILIZING THE CREATIONS OF THE WORLD. He put His divine power into action to heal all manner of sickness, to feed the hungry, to raise the dead, to cast out unclean spirits and demons, to deliver His people, to bear witness to His power, and to get the attention of mankind.

In the book of Numbers, there is a story of the prophet Balaam and a donkey. It demonstrates God's mercy and divine power to protect His people from destruction and death. It also reveals man is too often prone to sinful lusts and rebellion. Even when we fall prey to divers temptations, God will provide a way of escape.

Balaam entertained an evil deed that was contrived by a wicked king named Balak, king of the Moabites. The Moabites were a pagan tribe descended from Moab, the son of Lot. King Balak summoned Balaam to pronounce a curse on the children of Israel in exchange for a diviner's fee or a lucrative reward and honor for his services. King Balak feared the Israelites exceedingly because he recognized God was with them. The Israelites were a powerful people because of their faith in God, Jehovah; plus, they were numerous, and Balak knew what they had done to the Amorites. They were chosen by God as the people of a special covenant. Plus, they were unconquerable. God told them He would bless them and their descendants. If they were obedient to His Word, others would fear them.

King Balak wanted Balaam to curse the Israelites so he could overthrow them and drive them out of the plains of Moab. When Balaam was first tempted by King Balak's princes, he refused the diviner's fee. He also refused to accompany the princes of King Balak to their land because God spoke to him, saying, "Thou shalt not go with them" (Numbers 22:12). However, God also said, "Thou shalt not curse the people: for they are blessed" (Numbers 22:12). Just as God spoke to them, He speaks to us. We are to obey God and do whatever He asks of us.

King Balak yet again sent princes, more honorable than the first. He offered more to Balaam to get him to do the wicked deed. Evil always tries to get man to violate the Word of God. Balaam entertained the sinful deed with a proposition to the princes of King Balak to give him his house full of silver and gold. God spoke to Balaam again but told him to go with the princes of King Balak to their land. God's anger was kindled toward Balaam because He knew Balaam's heart and intentions. Furthermore, Balaam would not obey His first command to not go.

Therefore, God allowed Balaam to make his own decision to accompany King Balak's princes.

Balaam was rebellious and went with the princes for his own purposes and not those of the Lord. Even though God's anger was kindled, God's love and mercy overshadowed His wrath to protect Balaam from being slain. God's way to teach us His ways goes the limit to forgive us even though we fail to obey. Could this be because He uses us to fulfill His plan even if we act in disobedience? God's people should never allow the lure of money to divert us from the Lord.

Look at God's Unusual Way, With a Donkey, to Reach the Prophet . . .

While on the road with the princes of King Balak, God intervened by allowing Balaam's donkey to see the Angel of the Lord standing in the way with a sword. Only Balaam's donkey could see the Angel. Before God opened the mouth of the donkey to speak to Balaam, the donkey tried three times to discontinue the journey to save Balaam because he did not see the Angel. Balaam was angry and smote the donkey each time she stopped him.

God's love and mercy quenched His anger toward Balaam. As a result, He made the donkey talk to Balaam mouth to mouth regarding Balaam's offensive treatment of the donkey. What an amazing, strange occurrence between a donkey and a man! This is one of those times when we get to see God's divine power in action but in an unusual way. A donkey acknowledged God, and a prophet could not spiritually see because he was disobedient to God. How uncanny! How supernatural! That is the power and mystery of God. God knows how to get our attention to keep us from destruction, death, or perhaps worse: falling into the trap of the enemy. The Lord opened the eyes of Balaam. Indeed, he saw the Angel, bowed down his head, and fell on his face. Thus, Balaam professed he had sinned. God did not want Balaam to die at that time, so His divine power and hand of mercy were put into action to protect him.

This story reveals lessons to be learned and is relevant to how we behave today. One paramount lesson we should learn is to obey the voice of the Lord. God is moving in the earth today, yet it appears we cannot see His presence. The world needs the Lord to open its blinded eyes to its frailties. There are blessings and safety in obedience to God. He loves us and wants to protect us from all evil. God is our impenetrable shield. If we love the Lord with all our heart, soul, mind, and strength and keep His statutes, there is no good thing He will withhold from us.

For the Lord God is a sun and shield: the Lord will give grace and glory: no good thing will he withhold from them that walk uprightly. (Psalm 84:11)

Look What God Tells His People When They Obey . . .

God told the Israelites if they would keep His statutes and hearken diligently unto the voice of the Lord, He would bless them. Furthermore, their blessings would overtake them. Take a look at the Scripture:

> And all people of the earth shall see that thou art called by the name of the Lord; and they shall be afraid of thee. And the Lord shall make thee plenteous in goods, in the fruit of thy body, and in the fruit of thy cattle, and in the fruit of thy ground, in the land which the Lord sware unto thy fathers to give thee. . . . And the Lord shall make them the head, and not the tail; and thou shalt be above only, and thou shalt not be beneath. (Deuteronomy 28:10–11, 13)

As God's blessings were with Israel when they obeyed His commandments, they will be with us today if we obey Him. God's blessings were yesterday. God's blessings are today. And God's blessings will be forevermore.

Just as Balaam did not want to stop on the road while riding his donkey, our world doesn't want to stop to hearken unto the voice of the Lord. Because of that, our world is plunging deeper and deeper into the pit of darkness. And only God can save us from Satan's pit of darkness.

Look how God used a donkey to speak to Balaam to get his attention, but also look how Balaam was protected by God. In the same way, God is speaking to get our attention to save us from our sins and to come to the knowledge of the truth. He speaks to us in mysterious ways so that we may know Him and trust Him. Think of all the ways He speaks to us! God speaks to us through His Holy Spirit to guide us into all truth and in visions to give us direction, and He gives us clear pictures of His plan. He also speaks to us through His holy servants just as He used His prophet Samuel to tell Eli the priest His judgment. God speaks to us through warnings and wrath, which our world is experiencing today. However, the most powerful way God speaks to us is through His written Word. The question is this: Are we listening? Are we surrendering our will to His Will? Are we obedient to His Word? God's Word is true and is the path to righteousness and eternal life. We must stay in His will or we'll be in His way:

For the word of God is quick, and powerful, and sharper than any twoedged sword, piercing even to the dividing asunder of soul and spirit, and of the joints and marrow, and is a discerner of the thoughts and intents of the heart. (Hebrews 4:12)

Our world is experiencing devastation and reaping the consequences of disobedience. God is speaking and warning our world with painful curses, yet our world will not give ear to the voice of God. Just remember, "The Lord shall send upon thee cursing, vexation, and rebuke, in all that thou settest thine hand unto for to do" (Deuteronomy 28:20). After all, disobedience brings much sorrow and death. But obedience to God's Word brings peace and healing in the land.

What Is God Saying to Our World?

Hear now this, O foolish people, and without understanding; which have eyes, and see not; which have ears, and hear not. (Jeremiah 5:21)

It's like I can hear God saying to us today:

I created you in My image, but you are a world that has rejected me and forsaken My Word. I gave you My only begotten Son that you may have eternal life, but you have chosen the road of destruction and death. I gave you a world of beauty and abundance, but you have destroyed it with your wickedness. You are a world that is stiff-necked and uncircumcised in heart and in ears—a world that doesn't want to stop and heed to My Word or to My warnings. Must I resurrect the donkey that helped Balaam because you will not follow My Word? Oh, can't you see death on your road of darkness?

Why do you choose Satan's dark pit of torment when I and only I can give you light? Why do you choose hate when I love you and command you to love each other? Why do you choose disobedience when there is safety and blessings in obedience to Me? Why do you choose sin of sickness and suffering when there is healing and deliverance in Me?

Are you understanding the biblical truth I am trying to convey? If a donkey can see God's warning, why can't we? Can't we see we are in a world that is troubled? Are we blind to the conditions of this world? We are in a world of questions but choose not to go to Him, yet He is the answer, the way, the truth, and the life! For His Word says, "Come unto me, all ye that labour and are heavy laden, and I will give you rest" (Matthew 11:28).

Our world continues to circumvent God by using its own ability. Human ability can destroy life when it is not according to the Word of God, "for the wisdom of this world is foolishness with God" (1 Corinthians 3:19). Even in our disobedience, God gives us the opportunity to change because He doesn't want us to live a life of sin and shame; nor does He want us to perish in darkness. God wants to renew our hearts and minds and free us from sin and bring us into His fold to be a shining light for the world. God is a God of love, mercy, and forgiveness. He loves us, and He wants us to love and obey Him.

How Do We Reach God?

The only cure for sin—and the way to God's eternal glory—is through repentance. Repentance is the sincere confession of sin and the act of turning away in the mind and heart from the self to God. Repentance is far greater than man's ability to reach God. Repentance is the vaccine of salvation, forgiveness, and hope. It is the vaccine of healing and blessings. It is the vaccine of understanding God's far-reaching love toward us. It is the way to building a true, loving relationship with God and each other.

The world needs to kneel before God, our Creator of life, with an attitude of sincerity, humility, and reverence to God. When we pray, we must be as the publican and not the Pharisee, who was self-righteous:

And the publican, standing afar off, would not lift up so much as his eyes unto heaven, but smote upon his breast, saying, God be merciful to me a sinner. I tell you, this man went down to his house justified rather than the other: for every one that exalteth himself shall be abased; and he that humbleth himself shall be exalted. (Luke 18:13–14)

God doesn't want us to perish, but we perish because we will not turn to God. Remember the following:

The Lord is not slack concerning his promise, as some men count slackness; but is longsuffering to us-ward, not willing that any should perish, but that all should come to repentance. (2 Peter 3:9)

The world must not be as Balaam was with the donkey. Balaam was angry—just like the world. Brothers and sisters: anger will destroy, but God's love will heal! God's Word tells us He will forgive our sins and heal the land if we turn from our wicked ways and seek Him (2 Chronicles 7:14). The answer is waiting with arms open wide to receive us. Jesus is waiting. Let Him come into your life! Again, I must ask the question: If a donkey can see God's warning, why can't we?

The greatest lesson we can take from this story is that there is no power greater than the power of God. What

God blesses, no man can curse. What God puts in motion, no evil force or man can stop. There is no defeat in God. And if God is with you, there is no defeat in you.

Christians must remain prayerful and trust God and be a witness of God's Word in times like these. Trust His Word:

> Therefore, my beloved brethren, be ye stedfast, unmoveable, always abounding in the work of the Lord, forasmuch as you know that your labour is not in vain in the Lord. (1 Corinthians 15:58)

What Does This Mean to Us Today?

God is speaking to us and shaking this world. His handwriting is on the wall. He is moving. We cannot see and understand His mighty works because we are spiritually blind, but God is long-suffering, merciful, and full of grace. He wants us to be on His road of righteousness and not Satan's road of destruction and death. Let's seek Him and repent so our eyes, ears, and hearts will be inwardly circumcised with His love and to a life of obedience. When we are obedient to God, we will reap His blessings and be in His arms of protection. We will love each other as God loves us.

Our Prayer

Heavenly Father,

We come to You with a heart of repentance. Have mercy on us, Father, and forgive us of our sins. We have rejected You out of ignorance and disobedience, but we need You. You are our Creator, and You know what we need. Open our eyes that we may clearly see the path You have instructed us to walk in order to save us from a life of darkness. O Heavenly Father, create in us a clean heart and renew the right spirit in us so that we may serve You with a holy life and walk in Your Light—Your beautiful light! Thank You, Father, for protecting us from self-indulgence and from the road of evil. May Your Holy Spirit give us the control we need. In Jesus's Name we pray.

Amen.

Spiritual Seasoning

In the Word of God, faith is compared to a grain of mustard seed.

And Jesus said unto them, Because of your unbelief: for verily I say unto you, If ye have faith as a grain of mustard seed, ye shall say unto this mountain, Remove hence to yonder place; and it shall remove; and nothing shall be impossible unto you. (Matthew 17:20)

Why the mustard seed? To begin, the mustard seed is an amazing symbol of growth. Just think of all the possibilities of what a seed can turn out to be! There is much mystery there. Many consider it the greatest among herbs. Plus, a mustard seed is considered the smallest of all seeds, yet it grows to be a great naturally resourceful tree. Its start may have insignificant beginnings, but over time when it is fully grown, its outcome is purposeful, as it may yield beauty, provide many essential nutrients for nourishment, have medicinal purposes, and serve as a feeding and lodging place for the wildlife of

God's creation. In the spiritual realm, the mustard seed holds great significance as it will forever be remembered as part of Jesus's parabolic teachings of faith and growth.

On one occasion, Jesus taught this parable:

> Another parable put he forth unto them, saying, The kingdom of heaven is like to a grain of mustard seed, which a man took, and sowed in his field: Which indeed is the least of all seeds: but when it is grown, it is the greatest among herbs, and becometh a tree, so that the birds of the air come and lodge in the branches thereof. (Matthew 13:31–32)

Indeed, the mustard seed's beginnings are seemingly insignificant, but the seed has the potential for prodigious growth with proper conditions and care. To reach maturity, a mustard seed depends not only on human ability and care, but also on God's design—both naturally and spiritually. Yes! He is the Creator of life. So it is with faith!

Our faith may begin as small as a mustard seed, but over time, as we immerse ourselves in God's Word and form a loving and trusting relationship with Him, our faith will resemble the growth of the mustard seed. Faith depends on an individual's willingness to completely trust God, but more importantly, it is God who helps us grow that faith. At the same time, our roots must be firmly grounded and connected to the True Vine, Jesus Christ, so that our faith can be established. Undoubtedly, we are "rooted and built up in him, and stablished in the faith" (Colossians 2:7).

A mustard seed can produce substantial change in the earth as faith can bring forth unlimited change in human life. Faith is a divine tool that moves God's hand to people who believe. It is one of the great virtues that allow us to share in God's glory and nature. Faith works in the heart, for with the heart we believe, and transforms the mind, for the Word of God tells us to be transformed by the renewing of our minds (Romans 12:2). Furthermore, faith drives our will to do the will of the Lord.

Jesus knows the measure of our faith. He knows the heart, mind, and will of every human being. He does not demand us to have an abundance of faith to reach Him. He tells us just a little faith as a mustard seed will bring great reward. As proclaimed in the Gospel, faith the size of a mustard seed can move a mountain; hence, no matter how small or great, faith is what moves God to take action on our behalf or in our lives. During Jesus's ministry, He often said to those He delivered or made whole that their faith was the catalyst for their transformation:

And he said unto him, Arise, go thy way: thy faith hath made thee whole. (Luke 17:19)

Why is faith necessary in a believer's life? God's Word tells us that without faith we cannot please Him (Hebrews 11:6). Without it, we do not give God the opportunity to perform His wonders in our lives. With faith, we are putting our trust in God and believing that all things are possible to them that believe. Consider the following Scripture:

Jesus said unto him, If thou canst believe, all things are possible to him that believeth. (Mark 9:23)

Faith is a spiritual fruit we must possess to activate God's power and to show others our unwavering confidence in God. Faith represents God's Spirit working for us and in us. With faith, we believe that Jesus Christ is our Savior and that He gave His life so we may have eternal life, and have it more abundantly. Faith is our assurance that if we abide in Him and He abides in us, we shall reign with Him forever and ever.

CHAPTER 3

Faith of a Mustard Seed and a Touch by Faith in the Press

And he said unto her,
Daughter, be of good
comfort: thy faith hath
made thee whole; go
in peace. (Luke 8:48)

In Luke 8:43–48, the story of the poor woman who had been bleeding for twelve years is a testament of Jesus being moved by the woman's faith. This woman was afflicted with a perpetual disease, but like many people today who are suffering and dealing with illnesses and challenges, she had done all she could do. She'd spent her life on treatments with physicians with no results or deliverance. She felt not only was her physical state hopeless, but her mental state and social life were under a debilitating strain. She had twelve years of her social life ostracized as she was declared ceremonially unclean due to her blood condition. She was not permitted to enter the temple for twelve years because anyone she touched was declared unclean. Can you imagine? Twelve years of coping with the daunting pressures of life? A life filled with waking, painful nightmares? She felt nothing would work to change her situation or make life better. In fact, she continued to decline. Her mental state of mind was spiraling down into the valley of hopelessness. She was facing a mountain that needed to be removed. She was desperate for her miracle as change seemed impossible.

With her blood disease lasting more than a decade, she had to be frustrated and ashamed, weary and wounded, isolated and unclean. She felt like she had lost all hope. She was lonely and couldn't have any true relationships.

She didn't feel like or look like a normal woman. No doubt, she was ridiculed because of her putrid body odor. How many of us can relate to her desperate situation? How many of us have felt like giving in to our difficult situations from which it seems hard to escape? How many of us can empathize with her agony and suffering?

We often lose hope and give up on life when tribulations confront us. We lose hope with news of chronic or terminal illnesses and diseases. We lose hope with the news of tragedy and death of our loved ones. We lose hope in relationships. We lose hope in marriages. We lose hope with our family. We lose hope with love. We lose hope with our dreams not becoming reality. We lose hope because of extreme poverty or financial difficulties. We even lose hope in ourselves. Many things cause us to lose hope and wonder, *Will a miracle or change ever become a reality?*

But we must not succumb to a mindset of defeatism and hopelessness. We must not succumb to a life of incredulity. There is an answer! Life doesn't have to end with surrendering to defeat because our hope can be renewed with faith in Jesus. Jesus is the answer! Our life can be changed with faith as a grain of mustard seed.

One day, the woman with the blood disease heard great news that Jesus was in town. Her hope was renewed with the news of Jesus. This was her opportunity for her mountain to be removed to yonder. Her faith was greater than her condition, and this was her day for a miracle! It was her day to be healed—a victorious day that would change her life forever. Obviously, after twelve years of suffering, she was desperate for a miracle, so she acted on the news by putting her faith into action to find Jesus. Her mind was made up to go to her long-awaited answer, Jesus. She was determined to find Jesus, even in the midst of a crowd. She encouraged herself to press through the crowd despite her feeble body. She knew she was declared unclean, but that didn't stop her faith. This woman was challenged with pushing and pressing her way through the crowd to get to Jesus.

As she made her way through the crowd, she believed that if she touched Jesus's garment, she would be healed. She would be healed of her fountain of blood. She would be delivered of her unclean plague. She would be freed of her suffering. She had to step out in faith to get her great reward. What she did is what we all should do when challenged with the maladies of life: to be conquerors in Christ. She pressed through the crowd and came behind Jesus and touched the hem of His garment. As a result, she was instantaneously made whole! Her miracle happened, and her life changed. What a glorious day for the woman! Hallelujah! Jesus told the woman that her faith made her whole.

That woman's healing is a testimony of faith in God. Jesus did what no physician or any other power could do. Jesus didn't talk about the size of her faith in the crowd. He knew her faith. He said, "Who touched my clothes?" (Mark 5:30). With one touch of faith, in an instant, Jesus gave her life back whole. Faith as a grain of mustard seed can move God to action.

That woman touched Jesus with her faith, and we can touch Him with ours. Just as she put her faith into action, we must make up in our minds and hearts that we need Jesus to overcome our mountainous problems and afflictions. Brothers and sisters, take a step of faith! God wants to put His power into motion and meet the needs of His people. But we must trust and believe that He is capable of doing the impossible. Jesus is in town today. He is a touch away. He is waiting for us to touch Him with our faith. Trust God today with faith as small as a grain of mustard seed. Press through whatever you are facing, and touch Jesus with your faith. This is your day and time to be made whole.

What Can God Do With Our Faith?

Faith is the only hand that can take from God's hands. Faith always moves God's heart. Our faith is our connection with God and His connection with us because of our trust and belief. God takes our faith and shows us how to live a victorious life with Him. He takes our faith and opens our minds and hearts to a life of truth. Our faith gives God the opportunity to do something miraculous in our lives. Our faith moves God's hands to our hands. God can put special gifts in our hands through our faith.

Open your hands with faith and receive what God has for you. God used a rod in Moses's hand to demonstrate His power and wonders. Unlock your hands with faith. You can't see it; just believe it and receive what is yours from God. Through faith, God will use your hands for His divine purpose. He will supply our needs through faith. Simply put, just as children have faith in their parents to take care of their needs, we must have faith in our Heavenly Father to take care of all our needs:

> But my God shall supply all your need according to his riches in glory by Christ Jesus. (Philippians 4:19)

Without faith, we tie the hands of God. When we don't believe, God is displeased because He can do no works. God does not need anything to work miracles. However, faith allows the individual to learn the power of God by using his faith in God. Unbelief is rejecting the divine will and power of God. Unbelief is rejecting a relationship with Christ. And there is no relationship more precious and pure than our relationship with our Savior, Jesus Christ. When we go to God with our faith, He promised to reward them that earnestly seek Him. Move God with your faith.

What Does This Mean to Us Today?

Throughout the Word of God, we find that God performed mighty works and miracles through people's faith. We must understand today that God is able to perform miracles through our faith. He is able to heal through our faith. He is able to deliver through our faith. He is able to set the captive free through our faith. He is able to work in our lives through our faith. God is not asking us to have a great measure of faith; He said to us faith as a grain of mustard seed is enough.

Our Prayer

Heavenly Father,

You have the power to make the impossible happen. You have the power to make us whole and change our lives for the better like You did with the woman with the blood disease. You know every one of us and all of our needs, and You are able to meet them. You promised to supply our needs if we diligently seek You. Help us, Father, to seek You, to trust You, to love You, and to come to You with enough faith to receive our great reward. Help us to overcome our fear and doubt. Forgive us for our unbelief and rejecting Your divine will. Thank You, merciful Father, for Your love and forgiveness. In Jesus's Name we pray.

Amen.

Spiritual Seasoning

Who is our true Bridegroom? Jesus Christ is! Let us rejoice in this truth! Are we preparing to meet Him for that glorious ceremonial marriage? Will we be dressed in our spiritual garments to be received by the true Bridegroom? He is the only Bridegroom who can freely offer us a union of eternal love and life. He is our endless love. Oh, what a beautiful spiritual wedding it will be.

One of the parables Jesus used in His ministry referred to Him as the Bridegroom awaiting His bride (the Church). The parable compares the Kingdom of Heaven to ten virgins who took their lamps and went to meet the Bridegroom.

Then shall the kingdom of heaven be likened unto ten virgins, which took their lamps, and went forth to meet the bridegroom. And five of them were wise, and five were foolish. They that were foolish took their lamps, and took no oil with them: But the wise took oil in their vessels with their lamps. While the bridegroom tarried, they all slumbered and slept. And at midnight there was a cry made, Behold, the bridegroom cometh; go ye out to meet him. Then all those virgins arose, and trimmed their lamps. And the foolish said unto the wise, Give us of your oil; for our lamps are gone out. But the wise answered, saying, Not so; lest there be not enough for us and you: but go ye rather to them that sell, and buy for yourselves. And while they went to buy, the bridegroom came; and they that were ready went in with him to the marriage: and the door was shut. Afterward came also the other virgins, saying, Lord, Lord, open to us. But he answered and said, Verily I say unto you, I know you not. Watch therefore, for ye know neither the day nor the hour wherein the Son of man cometh. (Matthew 25:1–13)

This powerful parable stresses the importance of constant spiritual preparedness and faithfulness in the life of a believer to be ready to meet the true Bridegroom, our Lord and Savior, Jesus Christ. The true Bridegroom (Jesus) and His bride (the Church) illustrate a spiritual marriage or a nuptial covenant between Jesus Christ and those who have accepted Him as their Lord and Savior.

We celebrate many precious moments in our lives. These sacred times warm our hearts and bring tremendous joy and happiness. Most people would agree a wedding ceremony is one of the most special moments in anyone's life. It is a day filled with great expectation with the joining of two individuals becoming forever as one—forming as one flesh in heart and soul with a union of love, commitment, trust, and respect. Not only does it bring together the bride and groom, but it also unites their families and friends to witness an enchanting day. The most important and beautiful spiritual aspect of marriage is that it is ordained by God and "is honourable in all" (Hebrews 13:4).

A grandiose wedding ceremony requires a great deal of time, planning, and preparation. Although it can be arduous and frustrating at times, it is worth it in the end because the moment the beautiful bride enters the cathedral, everyone is mesmerized by her loveliness. While "Here Comes the Bride, All Dressed in White" plays softly in the background, the groom is at the altar eagerly waiting to take her hand in holy matrimony. What a joyous ceremony of love and togetherness!

There is no question that the ceremony of marriage is a pivotal, life-changing event. It is a beautiful picture of an inseparable union that God joins together. Even though marriage is a divine blessing, it is also a serious commitment of vows before God. After exchanging the vows, the couple begins a union with Christ as their foundation. God expects this union to be for life. Unfortunately, many couples end their earthly marriages in divorce, but that is not how God intended it. Consequently, this earthly marriage has much in common with our spiritual marriage.

Our earthly marriage foreshadows God's supreme, perfect marriage of the true Bridegroom: His Son, Jesus Christ, and His bride, the Church. Both marital unions are sacred and divinely created to fulfill God's eternal plan of love and life with Him and each other. He wants us to seek His guidance with both unions since marriage was established by Him. Plus, He knows what we need to prepare for what is to come.

Just as a bride prepares for her wedding, we must do likewise with our spiritual marriage. God offers us a greater marriage that goes beyond human life to eternal. He wants us to become one in the body of Christ through marriage with the true Bridegroom. If we can prepare for our earthly marriage to be beautiful, why wouldn't we prepare for and choose the perfect marriage with the greatest love of life? Just picture a marriage that is forever and more glorious than a traditional marriage and a typical human love story! A marriage that offers an eternal love and life with unlimited riches! A marriage into the holy royal family with the King of kings and Lord of lords to a pure and holy bride wearing fine linen! A marriage with a golden crown of glory and righteousness to be given to the bride! A marriage with the voice of the archangel and the trump of God sounding and the true Bridegroom descending through the heavenly clouds to get His bride! A marriage with love that shall never be forsaken!

My brothers and sisters, why wouldn't we choose a marriage with love that can give us ultimate liberty from death? Why wouldn't we choose a marriage with love that no human being could ever give? Don't we want a love and marriage like that? Do we want His love? After all, He loves us. He wants to be our true Bridegroom! And, one day, He is coming for His bride. For it is written: "Let us be glad and rejoice, and give honour to him: for the marriage of the Lamb is come, and his wife hath made herself ready" (Revelation 19:7).

Let the following question meditate in your heart and mind: Are we preparing for the greatest love and marriage of all? Behold, our true Bridegroom is coming! Remember: no one knows the day and hour, not even the angels of heaven, only His Father (Matthew 24:36). This eternal union is offered to everyone who believes and lives upright before the Lord.

We don't have to pay anything because the price has been paid. Jesus paid the full price on the cross that we may have an eternal union with Him. He laid down His life in love that we may have everlasting love with Him. Will we be ready for His everlasting love and that glorious day? Are we preparing with the right spiritual apparel? What are we wearing now to be ready for that day? Will our spiritual wardrobe be adorned with the beauty of holiness? Will it be adorned with the fruit of the Spirit? Will our hearts be full of love? Will our feet be shod with peace? Will our crown be sealed with truth? Will we have the covering of righteousness? Will we be ready as the five wise virgins, or will we be one of the foolish virgins who had no oil?

CHAPTER 4

The True Bridegroom Is Coming! Which of the Five Virgins Will You Be?

Watch therefore, for ye
know neither the day
nor the hour wherein
the Son of man cometh.
(Matthew 25:13)

THE PARABLE OF THE TEN VIRGINS IS A GREAT ILLUSTRATION OF HOW GOD'S PEOPLE MUST KEEP THE LIGHT OF GOD SHINING IN OUR LIVES. This parable has several important connotations and can be interpreted from different perspectives. However, one principal point is that we must live to be ready for the perfect spiritual marriage to come with the true Bridegroom.

The ten virgins represent believers of Christ. From some perspectives, the virgins were Christian women who were unmarried and had not had intimate relations with men; they were preparing for the true Bridegroom. But for this story, the virgins represent believers in the Church and the true Bridegroom represents Christ. They are those who are in the kingdom of the Lord. Their lives were changed because they had accepted Jesus Christ as their Lord and Savior. Therefore, if we accept Him, our lives will change from darkness to the marvelous light in the Lord.

The ten virgins were circumcised in the heart and transformed by the renewing of the mind. They were washed in the blood of Jesus. They were cleansed from all ungodliness and beautified in holiness. They were distinguished by the seal of the Holy Spirit on their foreheads and in their lives. However, as you will see, five of the foolish virgins were unable to celebrate a union with the true Bridegroom.

What a sorrowful day it was for the five foolish virgins! And what a sorrowful day it will be for those who are not ready for the Second Coming of the true Bridegroom. What happened to them can easily happen to us if we are not continuously preparing for His coming by staying in His good and acceptable will. Don't let your life keep you from entering the marriage, with the Lord saying, "I know you not" (Matthew 25:12). The choice is yours.

Preparing for the Kingdom of God begins with a new birth in Jesus Christ: becoming "a new creature: old things are passed away; behold, all things are become new" (2 Corinthians 5:17). We become brand new. Glory be to God! Only God can do that. Our sinful behavior has been forgiven, and we begin a spiritual daily walk on God's path of righteousness.

It is a walk of love and obedience to God's divine Word. We walk with God in His marvelous light as He has brought us out of darkness. Indeed, no more darkness for those who believe and live upright for the Lord. We cannot walk in darkness and walk with Jesus, for He is "the light of the world; he that followeth [Jesus] shall not walk in darkness, but shall have the light of life" (John

8:12). As born-again believers, we do not walk the wide path that leads to destruction and hell. We have chosen God's path—which is narrow and straight with truth and leads to eternal life.

What's so amazing about God's path is that you never walk alone because God will never leave you nor forsake you. Another beautiful aspect of this walk is that others walk with us as God binds us together in the body of Christ. We spread God's love and light to others. We share the good news of His blessings and miracles and that He is our wonderful Savior. We can walk His path together in love and in His beautiful light. His light will shine all around us for the world to see His glory.

In this divine parable, the five foolish virgins lost their light as their lamps were useless and they had no oil left in their vessels when the time had come for the great celebration with the true Bridegroom. Their lamps without light represent a life going back into darkness because the oil that they needed in their lives represents the Holy Spirit. They knew that the Bridegroom was coming, but they didn't know the day and time. If they had had God's Spirit in them, they would have been prepared and ready.

These five foolish virgins had lost their spiritual power to walk daily in God's Word and in His marvelous light.

They had so much spiritual loss, and because of that, they lacked wisdom and knowledge. They had no armor light for protection from a dark world or for the world to see God's glory in them. Their beautiful light was gone. They weren't preparing, nor were they ready in their spiritual wardrobe to meet Jesus. And what is so sad is that they didn't have time to get ready.

My brothers and sisters, we don't know the day and hour of the coming of Jesus. But God gives us every opportunity to prepare and be ready for our marriage with His Son, Jesus Christ. And He gives us every heavenly gift that we need to walk in His light with Him and get us ready for His coming.

God Prepares Us

God does not want us to perish, so He gives us what we need to live a holy and righteous life. He gives us the choice of free will and does not force us to live for Him. He loves us and has laid the foundation for our preparation with His divine power and gifts. Two of the most powerful divine gifts and powers that He gives us for preparation are His Holy Word and His Holy Spirit. God's Word and His Spirit agree together, so we must have His Word and His Spirit together. They both manifest the power and truth of the Father, the Son, and the Holy Spirit. His Spirit is the divine Author of all Scripture.

God's Word is our spiritual food for the mind, heart, and soul. His Word provides us a righteous path to live a moral and spiritual life. We need God's Word, for it "is a lamp unto my feet, and a light unto my path" (Psalm 119:105). The Word of God is infallible and shall stand forever. God's Spirit is our Comforter and teaches us to fully understand His Word and guides us in all truth. Jesus said, "But the Comforter, which is the Holy Ghost, whom the Father will send in my name, he shall teach you all things, and bring all things to your remembrance, whatsoever I have said unto you" (John 14:26). Also, remember God's Holy Spirit indwells every believer who walks upright before the Lord:

> And if Christ be in you, the body is dead because of sin; but the Spirit is life because of righteousness. But if the Spirit of him that raised up Jesus from the dead dwell in you, he that raised up Christ from the dead shall also quicken your mortal bodies by his Spirit that dwelleth in you. (Romans 8:10–11)

We have no power to live a righteous life without the Holy Spirit living inside us. Without the Holy Spirit, we wouldn't have power to stand against the evil of Satan. Without the Holy Spirit, we wouldn't have godly characteristics to transform us in the likeness of Jesus Christ.

God's Spirit produces the fruit of the Spirit in every believer. He gives us the fruit of the Spirit to help us walk upright in His image and to be a light of godliness to the world. Love is one of the greatest fruits God's people can bear. It was God's love for the world that He gave His only begotten Son that we may have eternal life if we believe in Him. The truth of the matter is this: everything with God centers on love. Just as God bestows His love upon us, He wants us to do likewise with Him and each other. Remember, the true Bridegroom is coming back for His love, the Church.

God gives us instructions to put on His whole armor to withstand the evil of Satan: the breastplate of righteousness, feet shod with the preparation of the gospel of peace, the shield of faith, the helmet of salvation, the sword of the spirit, and praying always (Ephesians 6:11–18). We need everything He has provided to walk His righteous path. God does not let us walk alone because He is with us to keep us strong. We can make it if we completely trust God with our lives.

What Does This Mean to Us Today?

God loves us and wants us to have a personal relationship with Him. To have a faithful relationship with Jesus is to gain everything He has promised in His Word. God's promises are faithful and true. Furthermore, God does not change. God has given us the opportunity to be in an everlasting, loving relationship that is pure and holy. With open arms, He takes us as a member of His royal family. He gives us everything we need to live for Him. And He promised He will never forsake us nor leave us alone. The choice to accept Christ as Lord and Savior is yours to make.

Don't put off until tomorrow what you need to do today. Don't always think you have time. Again, no one knows the day and hour of the coming of the Lord. Don't be like the five foolish virgins who didn't have time to get ready and get shut out of the great celebration with the true Bridegroom.

Sure, life these days is complicated. But when we walk with God, He gives us assurance of His presence and power in our lives. We have many things that cause us to lose our focus on Christ. Perhaps your faith in Jesus has been shattered by the struggles of life and your light is going dim and you have no more oil. Either way, now is the time to turn to God for help. Has your relationship with your husband or wife or family spiraled out of control and you feel there is no room for reconciliation? Now is the time to turn to God for help. Have you not accepted Christ as your Lord and Savior? Now is the time. Jesus is waiting to show you His love and compassion.

The five wise virgins got their eternal love and life with the true Bridegroom because they were ready. Having our names written in the Lamb's Book of Life is the greatest allegiance and promise we can have with God. Will God write our obituary with the words, "Well done, good and faithful servant" (Matthew 25:23)? It really doesn't matter what people say or what credentials we may have obtained. What matters is if you are right with God. Don't miss your opportunity to live for Jesus and to be ready for His Second Coming.

Our Prayer

Heavenly Father,

Thank You for Your beloved Son, Jesus Christ, our true Bridegroom. Jesus paid the price for the world to have the opportunity to be His bride. We need Your help to be ready for that glorious celebration. Help us to be a beautiful bride by walking Your righteous journey adorned in Your spiritual clothing. We don't want to be like the five foolish virgins. We don't want to run out of Your spiritual oil. Help us to keep our light burning because we know not the day or hour of Your coming. We don't want to live a life in darkness. Help us to shine bright for the world to see Your glory in us. We don't want to be foolish with our time in seeking You. Help us, Father, to utilize our time wisely. Help our spiritual mind to seek You and to be ready for that great day. In Jesus's Name we pray.

Amen.

Spiritual Seasoning

When the storms of life arise, we have two choices. We can be overcome, or we can be overcomers through the ultimate overcomer, Jesus Christ. Every one of us will encounter storms. This is a biblical truth. No one is exempt. Even Christ encountered His share of storms. They are inevitable and inescapable, but there is victory in our storms with Jesus!

In life we experience all kinds of storms. They do their best to overwhelm us, but if we can hold to our faith in Christ during the turbulence of life, we will soon overcome. In order to do so, we need massive survival skills. What do we do when our storms of life arise? How do we deal with their lingering consequences? Do we surrender? Or do we seek help? The answer is, yes: we do both by surrendering to Christ and seeking His help!

During Jesus's earthly ministry, He faced many storms, but He was the true exemplar of the ultimate overcomer. He overcame His storms to show the world there is no power and love greater than the Father, Son, and Holy Spirit.

Jesus accepted His earthly mission to overcome the sins of the world to set us free from the penalty of sin. Through Him, the power of death redeems us and reconciles us back to God. He arose victoriously over death, hell, and the grave with all authority in His hands. And, because of Him, our sins can be forgiven; if we repent, we can have eternal glory. His life proved that with God all things are possible. Consider the following:

With men this is impossible; but with God all things are possible. (Matthew 19:26)

He overcame His storms to show the world the only way to be a true overcomer of sin is through a life with Him as a born-again believer. He used the weapon of love and forgiveness on the cross to overcome His accusers when He cried out, "Father, forgive them; for they know not what they do" (Luke 23:34). Furthermore, Christ used the power of the Word and the Holy Spirit to overcome

Satan's temptations in the wilderness when He proclaimed, "Man shall not live by bread alone, but by every word that proceedeth out of the mouth of God" (Matthew 4:4).

Christ also used the weapon of prayer and fasting to overcome sickness and disease and to cast out devils. He was treated as a criminal but was clearly innocent; nevertheless, He overcame His suffering of persecution, betrayal, and rejection willingly to do the will of His Father. Jesus overcame the iniquitous things of this world for us. Finally, He wants us to be overcomers of the world to reign with Him for eternity. Jesus was unconquerable and victorious through His storms of life. When we accept Christ as our Lord and Savior, we are a new creation of overcomers. Praise the Lord!

CHAPTER 5

The Ultimate Overcomer, The Perfect Storm

These things I have spoken
unto you, that in me ye
might have peace. In
the world ye shall have
tribulation: but be of good
cheer; I have overcome
the world. (John 16:33)

IN THE BIBLICAL STORY OF THE GREAT STORM IN Mark's gospel, Jesus is with His disciples on a ship. He demonstrated His divine power in these spoken words: "Peace, be still" (Mark 4:39).

The wind ceased and the angry waves hushed. There was great calmness on the water. This was Jesus's "perfect storm" to show His disciples that all power in heaven and earth was given to Him. Moreover, this storm illustrated to the disciples that faith in Christ overcomes fear and doubt in the storms of life. Complete trust and confidence in Jesus will bring peace and victory in the midst of our squall.

Life will throw many storms at us. They can be unpredictable. Although we can have a notion that a storm is on the horizon, sometimes we never even see it coming. The unexpected drama can wreak havoc on the nervous system. In turn, we can experience various negative side effects that are enervating to the mind, body, and soul.

Some storms may be marginal, causing little damage. We might feel a little uneasy, but we know in a day or two everything will return back to normal. However, some storms may turn our lives completely upside down, and we may feel like we've been slammed by a hurricane with tempestuous waves tossing our emotions to and fro. Either way, storms can threaten our ability to think straight or make the right decisions. Some storms last longer than others and are like a constant thorn in the flesh that keeps us in a state of agony. Some cause catastrophic disasters that put us in a place of fear and hopelessness. Some may tempt us to harm ourselves and our relationships with others. Some are like turbulences that take us through a bumpy situation, causing major anxiety and sickness. Some are like a tsunami or tornado that can destroy everything in its path in just a matter of minutes, and the aftermath leaves us in devastation and standing in ruins.

Some storms act like a cancer that eats and kills all the good cells in the body. They may take us through more trauma like surgery, chemotherapy, radiation, and other painful medical treatments that are exhausting and draining. Others are like an alcohol or drug addiction. They don't take long to destroy relationships and damage our physical and psychological health. Furthermore, there are some storms we bring on ourselves because of our poor choices. They make us reap negative consequences. Although we sometimes create the storm and get ourselves into a sinful mess, if we sincerely confess our wrongdoings or sins to God, He will forgive us our sins.

Finally, there are storms that are preordained by God to build character, faith, and complete trust in Him. God allows hardships and tribulations to come upon us to make us spiritually stronger. These storms are sent to pour iron into our souls. God doesn't want us to have a weak and fragile faith, so He allows things to happen to make us stronger. For example, God allowed Satan to buffet Job for the perfecting of Job's faith, patience, and love for Him and to overcome his fears:

> For the thing which I greatly feared is come upon me, and that which I was afraid of is come unto me. I was not in safety, neither had I rest, neither was I quiet; yet trouble came. (Job 3:25–26)

Job overcame his fears and brought forth the Christian virtues all of us are asked to bring forth. Whatever God does, He does for our good, and He will see us through it.

Regardless of how the storms come, they can completely change the terrain of our lives. We may not be able to change a single storm, but we can choose to seek God's help to make it through the storm. God never promised us a life without storms, but He promised in His Word He will be with us to keep us in perfect peace and make everything work out for the good. Consider the following:

Unexpected Storms

And there arose a great storm of wind, and the waves beat into the ship, so that it was now full.

And he was in the hinder part of the ship, asleep on a pillow: and they awake him, and say unto him, Master, carest thou not that we perish? And he arose, and rebuked the wind, and said unto the sea, Peace, be still. And the wind ceased, and there was a great calm. And he said unto them, Why are ye so fearful? how is it that ye have no faith? (Mark 4:37–40)

The storm that arose while Jesus and the disciples were aboard the ship crossing to the other side was unexpected to endure. Sometimes, that is exactly how the storms of life come to us. They can hit hard and in a place where it seems inescapable and impossible to overcome. That is the "perfect storm" for Jesus to calm. Imagine the disciples resting in the ship out in the deep sea; Jesus was sleeping from a day filled with teaching a multitude that had gathered earlier by the seaside. All seemed to be well because Jesus was on the ship, but suddenly, a great storm appeared with tumultuous wind and raging water. The ship was swaying and filling with water. Everyone was in a panic! But just before all hope was lost, somebody had the sense to wake up the Master. Fear was the dominant emotion on that boat, and the way the disciples reacted to the great storm is the way we often react in our storms: fearful and faithless, wondering what to do or if we will perish in the storm.

The Questions

Who would want to be on a sinking ship? The disciples felt their lives were in jeopardy and they would perish. Even if they were the best of swimmers, it would be nearly impossible to swim to safety when the winds were blowing so hard. Besides, hardly anyone survives when they are ruled by anxiety and fear. God doesn't want us to muddle through our storms and drown. Why drown when we can live? We can read this story and judge them harshly, but wouldn't we be afraid if our lives were in jeopardy?

Why did the disciples doubt when Jesus was with them? Would we doubt with the ultimate overcomer, Jesus, with us? He promised in His Word He would never abandon us: "I will never leave thee, nor forsake thee" (Hebrews 13:5).

Why didn't the disciples believe Jesus was going to save them? They had seen all the good works Jesus had done. They had journeyed with Him and seen the miracles He performed. They had heard His teaching with parables to the multitude. So why were they faithless? More importantly, why do we mirror them during our own storms of life and become just as faithless as they were?

The Answers

We have to admit that we really don't know what we will do in the middle of a storm. My brothers and sisters, don't lose hope and faith in Jesus. He is the storm-soother! Jesus wanted the disciples to trust Him and have faith. He wants us to have faith in Him, too. What did the disciples do, even in their fear and disbelief? They went to Jesus. They knew He was their only hope, and we know He is our only hope. We have to do the same no matter what our negative thoughts, fears, and frustrations might be saying. We must go to Jesus!

We must go to Jesus especially when our storms bring us to tears. God sees and counts every teardrop. Tears are a language God understands. He hears our faintest cry. Storms make us kneel in prayer. When we fall down on our knees, God will put us on our feet in His strength to withstand the storms. We may stand on the Rock with our trembling feet, but the Rock never trembles under us. When we are going through our storms of life, we must seek the help of our Savior. Remember, brothers and sisters, "God is our refuge and strength, a very present help in trouble" (Psalm 46:1).

This is why the disciples went to Jesus where He was sleeping in the hinder part of the ship. They woke Him up and asked, "Do You not care that we perish? Save us!" (Mark 4:38; Matthew 8:25).

What a question to ask!

Jesus asked, "Why are you fearful? And where is your faith?" (Mark 4:40; Matthew 8:26). It is no wonder Jesus asked them this since they'd spent a lot of time with Him. We can relate to this, however. Do we not often find ourselves asking Jesus, "Why?" Do what ifs and whys usually plague your mind during times of sorrow, pain, brokenness, failed relationships, or difficult situations? Jesus knows our suffering. He is the suffering Savior. He experienced much sorrow and pain in His life on earth, and He showed us the right way to live through it. Turn to Him!

Jesus knew the disciples were petrified—He also knows our fears. He showed them His omnipotent power when He rebuked the wind and said to the sea, "Peace, be still." There was a great calm as the winds and sea obeyed Him. If we seek Jesus during our storms, He will say to our storms, "Peace, be still." In turn, our fears are resolved.

Sometimes in our storms of life we feel like no one cares and that Jesus does not hear our prayers. We take the position of giving in to the storm rather than seeking our Savior, Jesus Christ. Our storms of life are the "perfect storms" to save us and make us overcomers for the Lord.

What Does This Mean to Us Today?

Storms will always arise in our lives. Having Christ as our Lord and Savior doesn't mean we won't have storms. We must believe that our anchor is in the Lord and we have the power to overcome with Jesus.

Some of you are going through a rocky storm today. The tempest is raging! Your heart is heavy and troubled. It's tough. You can't think straight, nor can you see your way through the howling rain. The fact of the matter is, it is not for you to see, but the Lord to see for you.

When you feel like you are about to go under the water, focus on Jesus. He won't let you drown. You may feel like you are on the edge of the cliff, but hold on to Jesus's hand. Hold on! Hold on! Don't let go! There is victory on the other side of not giving up! You can make it! Your storm is His perfect storm to prove Himself faithful to you. Jesus calmed the storm for His disciples, so He will calm your storm today. Jesus will give you the power to speak, "Peace, be still."

Let's look at another example. We all can get inspiration from the life of King David with the many storms he faced in his life. Some storms he engineered because of his wrongdoing. And sure: we may do the same, but that doesn't mean we have to give up on life and God. Just do as King David did. He sought the Lord for forgiveness with a repentant spirit and asked God to create in him a clean heart and renew a right spirit in him (Psalm 51:10). The Lord gave the sweet Psalmist of Israel the most beautiful Psalm to comfort His people. Consider the following:

> The Lord is my shepherd; I shall not want. He maketh me to lie down in green pastures: he leadeth me beside the still waters. He restoreth my soul: he leadeth me in the paths of righteousness for his name's sake. Yea, though I walk through the valley of the shadow of death, I will fear no evil: for thou art with me; thy rod and thy staff they comfort me. Thou preparest a table before me in the presence of mine enemies: thou anointest my head with oil; my cup runneth over. Surely goodness and mercy shall follow me all the days of my life: and I will dwell in the house of the Lord for ever. (Psalm 23:1–6)

The Lord will be faithful to us. He will put a song of praise in our hearts and spirits to let us know we can be overcomers through Christ Jesus. He will calm the storm and calm us. We can walk in perfect peace no matter what storm we are in the middle of; even though "weeping may endure for a night, . . . joy cometh in the morning" (Psalm 30:5).

Our Prayer

Heavenly Father,

We give thanks to You for all things. We thank You for the beautiful sunshine and the storms of life. You didn't promise us a life without storms, but You promised to be with us in the midst of our storms. You said You would make a way of escape. Help us to understand that our storms of life arise to make us stronger and to build our faith in You. Without the storms, we wouldn't appreciate Your beautiful sunshine. Without the storms, we wouldn't know Your omnipotent power. Without the storms, we wouldn't understand the sufferings that Your Son, Jesus Christ, endured and overcame for us to be overcomers of this world. Father, You know our weaknesses and our frailties, but give us the mind to lean on You and Your strength to endure our storms because in You all things are possible. Help us to draw nearer to the ultimate overcomer, Your Son, Jesus Christ, so that we may be an overcomer for You in the storms of life. In Jesus's Name we pray.

Amen.

Peace Be Still

We are often faced with the raging storms of life

That bring tempestuous winds with rain fiercely beating
our lives.

Dark, ominous clouds hinder our view,

Making it unbearable to see our way through—

They cling like blustery waves, tossing us to and fro,

While we are trying to make it through, but they won't let go.

Those raging storms of life keep us in a fright,

But we must not surrender our faith during our stormy blight.

We remember the calming words of our precious Savior,
Jesus Christ,

"Peace be still," to the sea and wind. They ceased,

For our Savior is our refuge and will keep us in perfect peace.

He's the perfect Savior for your perfect storm.

In His loving arms, He will keep you safe and warm.

"Peace be still" to the sea and wind,

For our Savior is our refuge until the end.

Meet Lady Rochelle Williams

LADY ROCHELLE WILLIAMS comes from a large family. Her loving parents, James and Lillie Ross, raised seven children. Lady Rochelle is quick to give credit where credit is due. "Growing up in a large family could be difficult at times, especially with limited funds and resources, but that didn't hinder the love we had for each other. Still today, we are a close-knit family," says Lady Rochelle.

Her parents' strong work ethic shaped her young soul. She had a front-row seat to the countless sacrifices her parents made to support their large family. Their influence became part of who she is today. It was her desire to one day be a blessing to her parents like they had been to her and the family.

Lady Rochelle learned early to never give up on her goals and aspirations. However, she quickly realized having goals without God leading your path is like being a ship without a sail. After hearing her father-in-law, the late Pastor Alvin Williams, speak during a Wednesday night service at the Temple Church of God in Christ (COGIC) in 1975, she accepted Jesus Christ as her Lord and Savior. "God completely changed my life and the direction I was headed," she says.

Match Made in Heaven

When Pastor James Williams saw Lady Rochelle at the Temple COGIC, he felt the Lord showed him she would be his wife. And just as the Bible teaches in Proverbs 18:22, *"Whoso findeth a wife findeth a good thing, and obtaineth favour of the Lord."* Pastor Williams felt God had richly blessed him with a wonderful bride. They have been married for forty-seven years and have two lovely, talented daughters, Candice and Constance.

Since the very beginning of their marital union in 1976, Lady Rochelle has followed and supported her husband on the path that God led him. Though their path began at the Temple COGIC, God's will for them took the couple to the Homeland COGIC in 1978 and to the St. James COGIC in 1979. Lady Rochelle shares a little backstory:

On the road to St. James COGIC, Memphis to Brownsville, with two babies, was often taxing for me, but I wanted to stay on God's path for my family. When God directs your steps, it is designed specifically for you. He places you with the purpose of growing your seeds and helping others grow their seeds. St. James has been a path of many seeds: seeds of love, challenges, hard work, sacrifices, tears, joy, blessings, and so much more. I am truly thankful for all of it.

Lady Rochelle has labored in almost every area of the church and is currently serving as the president of the missionary board, which she has served faithfully for many years. She is truly proud of every board member and grateful to work with them.

Lady Rochelle is also passionate about tutoring young students because she wants them to be the best they can be. She says a little bit of patience and a whole lot of love make the difference. She is also building her spiritual podcast episodes through *Spiritual Food for the Soul,* a podcast of truth, love, and inspiration. She is grateful Pastor Williams has given her the opportunity to serve her church, and she appreciates his leadership.

Reaching a Goal—Delayed but Obtained

One of Lady Rochelle's goals was to attend college. She enrolled and attended later in life while raising her daughters, caring for her parents, and working her career. Though she had many sleepless nights, she managed to acquire her undergraduate degree, as well as a graduate degree.

Lady Rochelle's passion for helping people is why she chose to work in the Human Resource Management field for over twenty-five years. She has worked for several organizations in the Memphis area where she has been given many wonderful opportunities to work with community leaders, youth and young adults, seniors, and several non-profit organizations.

Her inclination for helping her community and working with her fellow Memphians doesn't stop with her being a Human Resources Consultant. She is listed as a Tennessee Supreme Court Rule 31 Mediator (Family/General Civil). She has conducted several pro bono family mediations in Memphis to help partners resolve conflictual issues.

To get away from the hustle and bustle of work, Lady Rochelle enjoys writing poetry. She feels her poetry is an expression of feeling, experience, and truth; it gives her the opportunity to write about life situations—good or bad.

Lady Rochelle's favorite Bible verse serves as her personal mantra as well as her vision for the future of the St. James COGIC. She feels there is much work to be done, and there is no time to waste. For this reason, she relies on the idea that *"the harvest truly is plenteous, but the labourers are few" (Matthew 9:37).*

Pastor Williams and Lady Rochelle feel truly blessed to be connected with a wonderful congregation. They both agree they are like family. "We love every member of our precious flock and pray God's unfailing love surrounds the St. James family," says Lady Rochelle. *Finally, she offers to each reader of this book the following blessing: "Beloved, I wish above all things that thou mayest prosper and be in health, even as thy soul prospereth" (3 John 2:2).*

It is by God's magnificent grace we get to call her not only Mom, but also our friend and confidant; yet most importantly, we call her a virtuous woman. As Proverbs 31:28–29 says, "Her children will arise up, and call her blessed; her husband also, and he praiseth her. Many daughters have done virtuously, but thou excellest them all." We are grateful to say our mother is the epitome of beauty, grace, and class, but it is her faith and trust in God that give us the fortitude to be strong on our Christian journey with the Lord. We are, because she is.

Forever love,
Your daughters,
Candice, Constance, and Queenie (grand dog)

www.ingramcontent.com/pod-product-compliance
Lightning Source LLC
Chambersburg PA
CBHW020329130626
46549CB00003B/1094